Born-Again Diva

From Phuck-You to Philosophy to Phixing the Arts Problem

Christine Fontana

VirginiaDiddit

Published by VirginiaDiddit in 2024
Melbourne, Victoria, 3000
www.virginiadiddit.com

National Library of Australia Cataloguing-in-Publication entry available for this title at www.nla.gov.au

Title: Born-Again Diva, by Christine Fontana
ISBN: 978-1-923221-01-7 (Paperback)
ISBN: 978-1-923221-00-0 (Ebook)

Cover design and typsettting: Christine Fontana

Cover image:
Copyright © Christine Fontana 2022;
being meaningful wasn't working out the way I'd hoped so I decided to give up painting [again], put my feet up and read a book, 2022;
acrylic on 2x canvas, 122 x 122 cm

CONTENTS

Phuck You (1)

Regardless of how nice he is or is not, I'm going to hate him. I realise this within the first week. He's my first gig as an NDIS Disability Support Worker, and – outside of piecemeal teaching gigs – the hourly rate is more than I've ever been paid. Finally I feel recognised for invaluable skills, the most important of which being that I'm a nice person, who happens to also be interesting-and-fun. Until now these intangibles have earned me no more than low-award wages in the shit-kickingest, labour-intensive jobs.

There'll be no shit-kicking with this job and I can't believe my luck. Since forever I've tried to arrange life so that I'm making art or writing all morning, and doing practical life things from mid-afternoon. At these rates I can manage this comfortably, enabling more effective use of my studio time.

The NDIS: society getting it right! People paid realistically for purely interpersonal skills! *Recognition! A revolution!* I believe at the time I've found the solution to The Arts Problem, which is as simple as creating a pool of arts workers and giving them support-worker shifts. *Good living! Plenty of time for creation!* This equals a balanced life that enables the genuine sharing of skills, financial security, and a naturalistic way of being in the world via our own communities.

I'll be the guinea pig. *I've got this.*

Then, reality hits. During my first shift I get an ominous taste of boredom, and a reminder of the line that exists between people who spend their time constructively and those who have time to kill.

But the real problems begin with Time-Flexible. With him and with every client since, the problems have always begun with Time-Flexible. *You can choose the session time, but it has to be one hour before lunch.* The role is Time-Flexible, *but you must be available every day*. If I say *let's try afternoons* (because it's Time-Flexible), I'm answered with: *no, I've gotten used to having my support worker here between 10 am and 2 pm, so it has to be 10 am to 2 pm. Make it any time that suits you, as long as it's 10 until 2*.

I make no art that first week, and not enough from then on. Every morning where I want to wake up into my studio and start working, my client's name appears on my phone with needs, activity suggestions, time changes. My concentration is shot.

He falls in love with me (of course he does), attracted to a kindness he's ironically stopped me from feeling. The care sector has so-far turned my biggest weakness into my biggest strength. As an interpersonal dynamo, *I love people!* Now, I also hate them. I look up from the desperately unhappy messages I've sent to friends, stunned by how un-nice I've become.

This shouldn't surprise me. My client's internal tempo is drug-buggered and frenetic. The motor tic I've spent my whole adult life managing – a barometer for stress that's more and more connected to anything that keeps me away from my projects – kicks into resistance. My brain is in torpor; my body tortured. Capitalism has done this. It's never been as clear to me as it is now: *I'm paid to fill up the emptiness of their lives, and to do so I have to subtract from the fullness of my own.*

My client is ten years my senior, so don't correct me (politically) when I tell you that after he started calling me *Mummy*, I started referring to him as *The Gimp*. It was all downhill from there. With the evaporation of my intrinsic loveliness I become, how you say, a complete cunt. My ability to disguise this new and evolving cuntedness is an essential skill for the position. I'm still lovely, don't get me wrong. But a cunt, yes. I am definitely, confrontingly, confusingly, that also. Because The Gimp is the enemy of art, and the seeds of anger have been planted.

Lovely? I am. *Until.*

Phalse Hope

The teaser to Australia's new National Cultural Policy, offered by Tony Burke just before the 2023 new year, invited something between a sigh of relief and an outright urge to celebrate the restored acknowledgement of art's critical role within society. Nevertheless, there was an air of suspicion accompanying the policy's anticipated release. Because without the adoption of the visionary changes suggested within optimistic arts practitioner submissions – feedback that was invited to inform the policy – it would simply contain *more of the same*. The risk was that restoring ten years' worth of eviscerated arts funding levels would be counted as "an improvement", rather than the starting point for real change.

I wrote the first draft of this essay in January of 2023, pre-policy-release, and post-pandemic. To be clear, I was writing from my position on the bottom tier of our creative population, after months of following the trajectory of those visionary ideas as they were being explored by arts professionals within public discourse. By offering my experience on behalf of all bottom feeders, I put forward the greatest test for the efficacy of this new policy; namely, if they don't reach people like me, the policy changes being developed are *not ambitious enough*.

The significance of the pandemic to this discussion cannot be emphasised enough. For the arts community [sector/industry/world], the pandemic was a landmark event, around which we now orient ourselves as a society.

There are those among us who were awed by the sociological possibilities arising from the pandemic situation. When the economy took a back seat the conversation was allowed to travel beyond fiscal practicalities and into philosophical ideals that called for social re-organisation. Covid-19 provided a circuit breaker, enough for imagining the impossible: capitalism's overdue reform.

Or at least it seemed that way, right up until the Coalition government attempted Humanities Murder, which undermined the essential nature of a vast section of the Australian professional populace, amounting to an assault on the organic nature of knowledge itself.

Not just through the new job-ready university fee structures that penalised students studying humanities degrees, but through the denial of pandemic support for arts and education sector employees, on which many arts practitioners rely.

With the government's help, capitalism had become the equivalent of a virus, evolving a new strain to counter the white-celled 'battle for change' the humanities threatened.

While that lack of support hit the nail in the coffin, Evelyn Araluen's 2022 Stella Prize acceptance speech hit a nerve:

> *Artists, in this country... are used to instability, we're used to two or three jobs, we're used to paltry super, and the constant fear of illness and accident faced by all precarious workers. We're used to living one pay-cheque away from poverty. Despite this slap in the face, this blunt dismissal of the clear social and cultural good the arts provides to all Australians, artists were still advocating and organising throughout the pandemic, and the fires and the floods. They were still working through the isolation of endless lockdowns in the hope that their creative efforts, their work, would help someone else survive.*

This public declaration of desperation and recognition of a depleted 'sector' resonated throughout arts communities for good reason. Around the same time, Alison Croggon was throwing down the gauntlet for the incoming Labor government with 'The Campaign to Destroy the Arts' – her essay response to the Coalition's 2022 Federal Budget. With justifiably angry cynicism she contextualises the value of the arts historically, and the viable challenge they present to governments:

> *Art tends to be anti-authoritarian. It argues against the simplistic. It opens possibilities. It values freedom. It imagines. Worst of all, it destabilises the idea of authority itself.*

Coalition attacks notwithstanding, throughout the pandemic it seemed to have been successfully argued that re-framing these as 'good' qualities is a hallmark of good society. Economics had finally met Philosophy, and somehow made friends with it. The purpose of this essay was and still is to hope out loud that we take this opportunity far enough to ensure that our tentative friend Capitalism is neither able nor tempted, in the future, to turn around and stab Philosophy in the back.

That the new policy was required for more than just pandemic recovery was evident in the introductory sentence of The Australia Institute's pivotal *Creativity in Crisis* report, which stated simply that *'decades of underfunding had weakened Australia's arts and entertainment sector long before COVID-19 hit'*.

I read the new National Cultural Policy (*Revive: A Place for Every Story, A Story for Every Place – Australia's cultural policy for the next five years*) after it was released in early 2023, first in long form and then the plain-English version, looking for signs of change that might reflect the optimism we'd naively let ourselves feel and articulate during this period.

It describes a dynamic arts sector that looks good on paper. The structural "pillars" supporting the new policy, which outline the various elements of arts sector reforms, in fact sound very reassuring at first glance.

But the devil is in the detail, and the dreaded more-of-the-same for us bottom-tier artists and writers is right there under *Pillar 3: Centrality of the Artist – Supporting the artist as worker and celebrating artists as creators*. Nowhere does this pillar – allegedly centralising the artist – discuss the need for ongoing financial security for individual artists. When it asks *how can we support artists as workers?*, the answer refers to employment that funds your practice; nowhere does it discuss art production itself 'being' the work for which artists are paid.

The competitive grant opportunities that offered the most significant support for an artist's practice before the pandemic (inadequately, let's say) remain in place. With, as feared, the funding that had been consistently cut by the Coalition government since 2014 being reinstated, but not increased.

Following up on this by scanning the list of individual artists awarded 'Arts Projects for Individuals and Groups' grants during 2023 – under Creative Australia's Visual Arts (just over 70) and Literature (50) categories – tells the whole story of same-old same-old for those of us who were hoping our "better futures" would finally arrive.

The lists aren't easy to navigate and therefore my counting isn't 100% accurate, but the 2024 grant recipients list under the same basic categories reveals similar numbers; [roughly] 62 and 58 respectively. These are the grants people like myself are likely to apply for, hoping for support of pure artistic production, as individual practitioners.

To call the grants *competitive* is an understatement, the laborious process of applying and the limited number of artists funded combining to create a dispiriting disincentive.

As Evelyn Araluen went on to say during her Stella acceptance speech:

> *The arts are only sustained, barely sustained, by unpaid labour. By the struggle and sacrifice of artists and arts workers who accept punishing and finally untenable working conditions for love and passion... This is not sustainable, and it never has been. This structure produces mass inequality of representation and will*

continue to restrict access for creatives from working-class and marginalised contexts.

A competitive arts scene isn't capable of supporting the growing demand for creative activity across our nation. It certainly offers no dignity to artists forced to beg for scraps. So for those successful 2023/2024 grant recipients, well. Good luck surviving on the variable (often tiny) amounts you were awarded.

This was the Death of Optimism, but were we really expecting anything else?

Invaluable = Undervalued

On the eve of Covid-19's arrival in Australia, Alison Croggon had already provided the "Before" to our post-pandemic ("After") situation, in her 2019 essay 'The Desertification of Australian Culture'.

A defining feature of today's Concerned Citizenry is the need to negotiate the hierarchy of

Things to Worry About when staking a claim for financial support. To clarify, arts practitioners are consistently placed on the defensive when it comes to having to 'justify' dedication to their craft, as though we're asking for charity and not a justifiable income. AC begins her essay with examples of global environmental abuse, circumventing any critical dismissal of what she explains might feel like a 'fatuous' discussion *'about Australian art and culture amid such overwhelming global crises'*, before launching into an astute analysis of the disintegrating state of Australian arts policy and support, and why it matters. On behalf of all of us she eliminates the need for these demeaning justifications with the correct but easily overlooked assertion that *'this global backdrop frames and influences what's happening to Australian culture'*;

> *The same ideologies that accelerate ecocide and political extremism are also destroying our cultural memory, starving our institutions and disenfranchising artists.*

This relationship includes what the *Creativity in Crisis* report likewise describes as the erosion of public investment in *'facilitating an arts sector... through decades of "market first" economic ideas'*.

Alison C laments the difficulty of making connections *'between cultural phenomena and the bigger picture'* in a society that easily dismisses the significance of the arts as sentimental at best, even as it lauds their invaluable contribution to Australia's economic prosperity. She succinctly articulates the ubiquitous nature of art within our social systems, which in turn explains the value of an artist's perspective on that "bigger picture":

> *...it's hard to trace the infinite complexities of how cultural fields interact with political, social and economic worlds... culture is simultaneously an artistic, social and economic phenomenon. And the vectors run in all directions: not just from top to bottom or bottom to top, but laterally across the topologies of all human activity.*

The endless struggle to redefine the value of

the arts outside of exclusively economic terms is exhausting and, frankly, like pissing into the wind, but with each attempt, more ballast is added to the weight of complexity underpinning the role of the arts in society.

More recently, in her 2023 essay 'Artist burnout is not a mental health issue it is a labour issue', Marisa Georgiou manages to create a bridge between professional creative activity and the 'ideologies of budget-balancing austerity', by conveying the essence of cultural influences as they trickle down through consumerism's paradigm:

> *[They] are actually incredibly valuable in an economy that no longer relies on the production of physical commodities as its primary mode of producing value. As media philosopher Franco "Bifo" Beradi points out, our economy now predominantly creates value by mobilising attention, which is driven by workers' creative, affective and communicative abilities. The artistic activity of creating new aesthetic trends, stimulating*

> *cultural engagement and producing new discourses is readily absorbed into a flow of immaterial commodities. The structures that channel them create wealth for property developers, media platforms and other corporate entities, but this is rarely seen by artists themselves, and far exceeds any financial investment made in them...*

There's no such thing as a homogenous human, but the market is a homogenising system that denies our right to play the role some of us are wired to play. When I read a news headline after the release of the new National Cultural Policy that quoted Prime Minister Anthony Albanese stating 'Arts Jobs Are Real Jobs', I rolled my eyes and whispered *fuck you*. That we live in a world where this needs to be announced is both offensive and devastating.

There are two ways of loving people. The interpersonal, and the abstract. Where on the ground I [sometimes] love to be around people, paid employment has taught me there's a limit. My mother's objective, through volunteer advocacy work, is to champion the voiceless individual. As an arts practitioner, mine is to contextualise individual experience within social systems in order to analyse, expose or encourage reflection. If you need a quick and lofty role to attribute to the "fine" arts (as opposed to the exclusively decorative and easy to commercialise arts), that role – moreso now than ever – is both to reflect and keep checks and balances on the status quo.

Our challenging-the-world methodology always begins with a determination to re-combobulate the discombobulating. What Alison Croggon and Marisa Georgiou are drawing attention to is the active quality of the arts/humanities in untangling the interrelation of all things, of which most arts practitioners are undoubtedly already aware. In addition to generating an ongoing supply of commercially pirated aesthetics, the arts are sociologically functional, provide a vital expression of shared ideologies, and encourage analytical thinking.

This latter point becomes more and more essential in a global society where misinformation threatens to destabilise social foundations.

This is a significant element of the business many of us are quietly and laboriously going about. Unrewarded.

Phuck You (2)

The Gimp had destroyed in a matter of weeks the calm I'd spent months restoring to my studio/ writing life. I'd achieved this by taking time off from paid employment and living off my savings (AKA eating into my mortgage). In market terms, we call this investing in ourselves. It takes courage to do this, and significant financial sacrifice.

During those months I'd made works that were shortlisted, exhibited, published, and awarded, illustrating the difference dedicated time can make to artistic focus. With my creative practices quietly flourishing (albeit temporarily and at a financial loss), I'd also prepared research that would see me accepted into a Creative PhD program.

The catch? No scholarship. I typically deferred worrying about it.

I wasn't prepared for the onslaught of interruption my NDIS work would invite. But something had shifted. My radar receptive, I was collecting incidents of artists, writers and philosophers facing financial obstacles across all ages. Everywhere you look, history is full of world-changing obsessions, individuals who answer callings and practise devotion to their craft or interests or both.

This is not a romantic notion. Every podcast, every essay, every book contained some casual reference to the struggle that needed to be overcome to create a work. Along with the struggle to survive came the artist's lament for the time they weren't able to utilise in the service of their goals, the subsequent loss we can only imagine.

Patrick White, on the other hand, was able to write full-time due to receiving an adequate inheritance at a relatively young age. Try imagining the Australian literary landscape without a Patrick White, and then *do the maths.*

As Virginia Woolf explains in *A Room of One's Own,* she was likewise able to write only because she received a sizeable inheritance, having stated clearly within the introduction to this seminal work that *'a woman must have money and a room of her own if she is to write fiction'*. The financial aspect, somehow, didn't make it into the frequently-referenced title.

They were the lucky ones. At the other end of the spectrum, I learn from a documentary that traces the provenance of a specific artwork that in at least one of his [dank] residences Modigliani slept on a mattress on the floor, surrounding it with water to discourage bed bugs.

My anger at this and many other stories was at first historical, then inconsolable, waking me from a feeling of deep shame for my inability to fit into the capitalist model. An artist, a writer, and with a debilitating introversion, I had a triple handicap and for decades had believed my situation was my fault. *There was something wrong with my character;* I was *lacking the competition gene;* I was *lacking ambition; unable to care enough about money; my introversion was a weakness.*

Shame is crippling, but at that point I had the single most important epiphany of my art-making life. The phrase I'd so commonly used to accept my lot – that *I was poor because I chose this;* that *I WAS NOT THRIVING BECAUSE...* – was turned on its head. The replacement phrase was so loaded it left me stunned:

I did NOT choose poverty;
I proactively chose ART(s).

The effect was galvanising, allowing me to reframe my whole history. Decisions I'd thought of as *bad decisions* had really just been *art decisions.* All of those situations where I was offered promotion or professional opportunity, but had walked away from advancement because accepting would have required I give up writing a novel or making a complex artwork. Each time, I chose the novel. I have always chosen the novel.

The Lottery Delusion

Watching *Framed* on SBS – a documentary about the 1986 theft of Picasso's *Weeping Woman* from the

National Gallery of Victoria – the 'ransom' demands made by Australian Cultural Terrorists (who claimed responsibility) seem in retrospect to be illustratively naïve. But regardless of how seriously you take the 'stunt' of the Picasso heist itself, with its larrikinesque audacity, the demand letters were consistent in their appeal to provide support for struggling artists.

Moving on from this almost slapstick action, we could say that the playful acronym of *ACT* has now morphed into Australian Cultural Theorists, to describe those who've picked up the baton and hope to take the campaign all the way to fruition.

These Cultural Theorists have a lot to unpick. The Australian arts landscape has changed dramatically since the late 80's, its sociological qualities elevated by educational restructuring and academic engagement, its practitioners enjoying a support explosion that would go through many economic iterations before it began to dissolve.

That 'support explosion' has morphed into a bitter pill. Sophia Cai, in 'When Should You Work for Free?', describes the *'romanticisation of artistic labour'* and the *'starving artist trope'* within a cultural sector in which the predominant support offered to artists takes the form of the aforementioned competitive grants system. This identifies one of the major impediments to surviving within the existing arts support model, and explains my pre-emptive (then fully realised) disappointment in the perpetuation of this system, enshrined in Australia's new National Cultural Policy.

> *The arts sector... becomes ripe for self-exploitation, as the onus is placed on the individual artist to keep trying.*

This relentless keeping-on-trying leaves arts practitioners dependent upon the mercy of what Marisa Georgiou (as quoted above) describes as The Attention Economy, within which *'our industry extracts its value from deeply human places, offers little in terms of stability or remuneration and erodes community support'.*

Emphasising the desperately extroverted prerequisites to succeeding within the competitive grants system, MG describes the selection criteria behind contemporary art commissions to illustrate how The Attention Economy works:

> *The development of temporary employment, funding and presentation models pressurised by attention-based KPIs of visibility, speed, volume and mass engagement drives the perpetual mandate of "new, now". This incentivises a constant, often panicked, flow of disposable artistic activity – a constant, often panicked, flow of disposable artists.*

In 2014 Affirm Press published *Funemployed*, a book lamenting the state of arts-life informed by the personal experiences of Australian practitioners who barely survive financially, even at the height of their success. Author Justin Heazlewood devotes some content to describing art's increasing reliance on social media as *'a peer-pressured social matrix [that] threatens to hijack an artist's creative brain'*. Whilst platforms like Instagram can (and do) provide a beautiful point of connection, at times it seems like a constant and exhausting avenue for forced performativity.

How this affects your output as an artist depends on your personality, but as JH suggests, we're *'now expected to tow the business line – being fully integrated with our audience while making fresh work'*.

As you can imagine, the reliance on social media presence for artists has been magnified in the ten years since. As MG explains, *'too many of us experience the pressure to remain socially visible as well as creatively visible, for fear that we may be forgotten by the constant flow.'*

In practical terms this points to the pressure to attract a significant public following before being taken up by galleries or publishers, or in order to be awarded your precious grant. In other words you're doing the marketing for your projects in advance, and are most likely to succeed if you're able to "arrive" before you've even taken your first step.

Anwen Crawford, whose essay *Decorum Serves the Rich* made a significant splash on the cultural landscape in 2022/3, provided us with a breath of fresh fed-uppishness by generously offering up the explicit and abysmal details of her own financial experience as a 'successful' arts practitioner. In doing so, she highlighted the added layer of difficulty for writers trying to survive within this external landscape. She describes an inverse process, or circular anomaly where the chicken and egg question takes on a new shape, because writing is *'a cumulative skill. You get better at it over time (in theory), and in order to get better at it, you have to put things out'*:

> *The publishing industry's relatively recent notion that everything – everything, including a writer's whole future career – rides on an artistically immaculate, brilliantly reviewed, best-selling debut is absolute horse shit, in part because it depends upon the commodification of the writer themselves. You, first-timer, are become the product to be sold, and you'd best believe that you'll be superseded when the new one comes along. Better to sidestep that crap as elegantly as you can, I think.*

Even as I watch my more extroverted friends take on the grants system with awe, I'm shocked by the struggle they face to make it work. Writing a grant application equals time not-spent writing novels or making art. Even if you're successfully awarded a grant, negotiating this minefield of complex beggary is often rewarded more with CV content than with income. Especially if you're a large-scale installation artist, where most of your grant money can end up spent on engineering approvals, materials, production assistance, leaving nothing to cover the cost of your 'labour'.

The immateriality of this kind of 'success' is mirrored in the competition scene. Where shortlisting and selection for art award exhibitions theoretically increases your cultural value as an artist, the monetary aspect of this honour more often than not results in 'anti-payment'. Meaning that, in addition to an entry fee, selected artists are usually not-paid for the inclusion of their work in award exhibitions, and in fact are themselves paying sometimes exorbitant framing and/or freight costs in order to have their work shown.

This is not the fault of institutions who run the award events (who are often underfunded themselves), but is rather a result of the accepted and faulty norms in which artists are required to be grateful for immaterial rewards, for the invaluable (and therefore un-valued) combination of labour/ skill/talent/investment that is being recognised through this award process.

This is the fine arts equivalent of Justin Heazlewood's "friend" likening *'the Australian art scene to the Victorian gold rush. Back then, the people who made the real money were the shopkeepers, taverns and hotels. Today, it's the venue managers, publicists, agents, poster companies and street press who are propped up by the dream dime'.*

It's little wonder Alison Croggon describes independent artists as *'exhausted' and 'pessimistic about their prospects'*, with *'less money distributed to fewer people'* each year.

After reading *Funemployed* when it was first released, I recommended this book to every-interested-body with missionary zeal, believing that *Funemployed* would do for The Arts Problem what Christopher Hitchens's *God is Not Great* would do for The Religion Problem (i.e. illuminate the absurdity, correct the aberrant ideological pathway, problem[s] solved).

Neither of those things eventuated. People still – incredulously – cling to religious beliefs, and arts practitioners still – incredulously – struggle. But what did follow were multiple formats (essays, podcasts, documentaries) encouraging individual artists to get their personal stories out there.

It's become clear that one reason preventing them from getting angry with the system is that it takes a long time for artists to stop believing in the Lottery Delusion, which fuels our dreams with the promise that if we work hard at our unpaid labour, we'll eventually be rewarded.

Lauren Carroll Harris marries this idea to talent in her essay 'The Case For Salaried Artists':

> *Artists are still being fed the individualism of the genius myth, that their talent will allow them to outpace the gig life, even as that myth has betrayed them.*

Sophia Cai, in relating her volunteer history, states that her success *'is marked by a realisation that I would almost certainly not be in my position today without these unpaid experiences, but also that these choices were only made because of the pre-existing expectations of doing unpaid work in our sector'*.

For others success doesn't arrive at all, and for others still, success does not equal living comfortably on their arts income.

Charlotte Wood's new National Cultural Policy submission gives us a clean overview of this situation, noting that before winning the 2014 Booker Prize, '*Richard Flanagan was on the verge of leaving Tasmania to find work driving trucks in the northern Australian mining sector*'. Before winning '*the Copyright Agency Fellowship and subsequently the Miles Franklin Award, Melissa Lucashenko had survived by being an Uber driver*'.

As Charlotte makes clear, one award will not guarantee financial security for a lifetime. Being on the lottery trajectory blinds victims to the fact that unless you win consistently, even awards don't guarantee indefinite support.

Here's a good place to mention that Melissa Lucashenko has since gone on to win seven more awards, for her novel *Edenglassie*. An article by Kelly Burke – published in *The Guardian* newspaper after

ML was awarded both the $100,000 ARA Historical Novel Prize in the Adult category and the $50,000 Margaret and Colin Roderick Literary Award within a 24 hour period – quotes the author saying *'I've made more money from writing within the past two days than I have in the past three decades'*. Demonstrating that even consistent award winning, apparently, does not a well-paid writer make. The prize of ongoing support for most artists simply doesn't exist.

Sociologists refer to the process of relying on an imagined but delayed reward as Hope Labour. If you're an artist you probably don't have to read beyond the abstract of Susan Luckman and Stephanie Taylor's 2023/4 essay 'There's a Lot of Luck Involved: Sustaining Hope Labour Amid Workplace Inequality and Precarity as a Creative Worker' to recognise your own psychology.

Here they describe creative "aspirants" as *'sustaining themselves through survival strategies variously theorised as 'hope labour' and 'aspirational labour'*, in order to explore *'how ideas of 'luck', 'chance' and 'opportunity' are implicated within such labour as sense-making resources for managing difficulties and justifying persistence in the face of precarity'.*

This is enough to alert us to the dangers of further reading on this subject if we wish to cling to our precious denial of the sad reality in which we operate. Because problematically, as artists we're doomed to accept continual struggle as a rite of passage, on our way to... *oh.*

Denial meets Reality

In 2020 I was one of twelve artists featured in artist Nina Sanadze's initial *Living Room* series – films contrasting artists in their home studio spaces with the paid employment environments that take them away from their 'world', emphasising their struggle to survive financially.

At the time I was "food lady" at a major hospital – an intensely physical job and my most successful stint at being a proper adult. I'd tried many strategies for surviving on well below poverty-level income for years on end in order to fund my studio/writing time, but instability/insecurity was closing in. I was entering the 'precarious female' age-group and needed to buy an apartment, before it was too late.

I both loved and resented my hospital job. Before the NDIS came along, kitchen work had seemed to me the first Solution to The Arts Problem. When combined with care roles (within aged-care or hospital settings), it provided an income with flexible hours that allowed for studio/writing time, and gave me somewhere to put all of that disgusting love. Theoretically, because it wasn't mentally taxing, I'd be able to leave my work at work, and keep my thoughts channelled towards projects.

Hah.

I remind myself often that I'm lucky I was able to buy an apartment, but the loss of time was punishment. I was squeezing life commitments and studio time into an inadequate few hours each morning, lifting my head at midday to quickly get ready and leave.

Lunch sometimes meant picking from my raw nut container. Cashews and walnuts are more effortful to chew, so for the sake of efficiency I'd go for the almost dissolving texture of macadamia nuts.

Because raw nuts, obviously, are the enemy of art.

If I had enough minutes I'd throw together some dry biscuits with avocado/bruschetta/goat's cheese, which I'd have to eat when I stopped at traffic lights on the way.

Eventually I stopped being able to justify the time it would take to tie my shoelaces, pulling them on pre-laced while rushing out the door.

Shoelaces, also, are the enemy of art, and my daily segues into normal life were unhealthily adrenalin-feulled and utterly graceless.

What Nina's films don't convey is the shame of submitting hastily finished work to publishers or competitions during that pre-shift panic. The constant, suffocating rush that makes this shame inevitable. Desperation. Insanity.

After discussion about median income for even successful writers, and couched in their overt and indisputable contribution to Australian culture and identity, Charlotte Wood's new NCP submission spells out the reality of employment:

> *Most writers I know have at least one and often three degrees. They are highly*

> *educated, highly motivated and highly skilled workers, but in order to make time to write they must accept work that is flexible, casual, part-time, freelance, poorly paid and precarious.*

Despite a modest award history, as a writer I'm perennially 'emerging', my perspective that of an experienced beginner.

The reality of a notoriously impenetrable publishing industry is beside the main point in this context, but the need to devote time to the writing and revision of multiple works, the need for immersion in the worlds we create, the years-long process of honing our craft, characterises the lifestyles of writers in my position. The cost of manuscript appraisals, of which we require multiples per manuscript, is prohibitive.

Loving your [shit-kicking hospital] job doesn't change the fact that being viscerally torn away from art and writing projects to "wash dishes" for a living is soul destroying.

Re/A/warding

For non-commercial artists who've all but given up on the temporary relief offered by the competitive grants system, there are other ways to get your work out there, each with their own associated disadvantages. For example, I rely on the aforementioned competition scene, which counters the necessity of self-promotion (my Achilles heel). I enter competitions in order to secretly join the world through the back door, hoping for quiet validation and a way to build a professional profile *without having to build a professional profile*. Award events allow somebody like me to exhibit/publish their work meaningfully and a little bit festively without having to organise (or endure) a solo show.

Justin Heazlewood's on my side when he says *'it's little wonder that artists find the concept of networking and self-promotion confronting, as industry demands are in direct opposition to their psychological design'*.

These days, shortlisted writers (of short works) are often anthologised. This contextualises "winners" within a thriving microcosm, celebrated among equally-worthy peers. As with award exhibitions, this does a great deal to foster the idea of community, leading some towards tentative action within their respective fields.

As a shortlist-ee for *Overland's* 2021 Judith Wright Poetry Prize, when I received the email informing me that I was NOT the winner, I was in the middle of running a temporary (grant-funded) community arts space with my ShrewD art collective peers. This ad-hoc arts space experience was revealing an overwhelming public hunger for points of connection, creative activity and interaction. It had triggered conversations about the inefficient nature of grants in places where more sustainable opportunities for both art and community-building were clearly needed.

In the midst of this charged enthusiasm for a possible *Future for the Arts* for *All Time*, I received another email, with a request made by the award winner, Ender Baskan:

> *My fellow shortlisted poets, I'd like to share my prize money with you. I hope you take*

this gesture as a simple act of solidarity amongst poets. I did not overthink the decision to do so, my poem called for it and after winning I had to follow through. If you read my poem it'll make sense. Thank you, Ender

I'd been carrying reminders of financial vulnerability about my person all week, but this presented me with a dilemma, because accepting the money would mean taking from a writer who'd earned that money on the merit of his work. Conversely, declining meant being excluded from the solidarity Ender hoped to foster.

What if Ender was also struggling? Had the ball joint also dropped from the bottom of his car as he went over a speed hump? Had his car window switches also stopped working, so that there was a permanent two-inch gap between the glass and the top of his car doors? How could I say no to something that so genuinely activates the call to unite?

On a personal level, Ender's wish to share was like a symbolic rescue. Beyond car fixing, though, the social level was more far-reaching. Ender may not have overthought the decision, but I clearly had. I accepted his offer, hesitantly buoyant with the optimism it generated, and survived the immediate future (at least two minutes of it) with a little less stress.

As with Carrie Tiffany sharing a portion of her Stella Prize money with other shortlistees in 2013, and Thomas Keneally sharing his 2022 ARA Historical Novel Prize, Ender's gesture will resonate as a bold and generous action. A call to something I would appreciate more fully when I finally read his winning poem.

Pathways

Not long after this experience, I made the decision to fully embrace my [perennial] failure by dropping out of the PhD program I'd so desperately wanted to join. I'd vacillated for months, struggling with motor tic management, juggling research with paid work, with studio, with *life*.

Seeking advice from my supervisors, one told me she'd handled the problem of being overloaded and overwhelmed by making a list of projects she'd abandoned before undertaking research, intending to return to them once she'd finished. When I asked if she'd eventually completed those projects, the answer was no, they'd somehow *fizzled out*.

Could I go six years without my projects? Without a workable income? Another six years of doing something I love, but doing it to the exclusion of things I love even more, and doing it unpaid?

Not just that, but doing it without a guaranteed career path at the end of it all?

The unattractive mathematics of this was reinforced by Jennifer Mills in her essay 'Precarious Words'. JM describes how the avenue of supplementing your income with tertiary teaching gigs – often adopted by artists and writers – has become an untenable prospect, due to the '*decimation*' of tertiary education itself, thanks to the Coalition '*government's frankly hostile approach*';

> *All of this is creating a class barrier to participation in literature, art, journalism and media that impoverishes everyone.*

I'd naively run towards the false security offered by a sector eroded by years of funding cuts, spuriously justified by capitalism's mindless push for ever-increasing efficiencies.

The catch 22 of evidential graduate earnings being used to justify the continuation of government support for tertiary humanities courses is artfully described in James Ley's 2021 essay 'Trapped in Negation'. Ley pinpoints the cyclical absurdity of measuring those graduate incomes within a system designed to destroy itself if subjected to capitalism's blind edicts. Effectively (and here I rephrase his point): we pay you less because capitalism told us to, and then we refuse to fund your courses because you're paid so little, which offends the glorious principals of capitalist success.

Defining what's at stake for humanity when a short-term government has the power to favour "job-ready" courses above qualitative research by brutally slashing funding, Ley identifies an apocalyptic assault on knowledge, and:

> *...a view of the world that is not merely philistine; it's been conceived in such a*

> *way that it's incapable of registering the value of any kind of meaningful abstract concept that speaks to our inner being or our collective existence. Not only truth and justice, but beauty, morality, society, and of course the proposition that an education in the humanities might have a value that has no valid metric, that its greatest value may well be that it refuses to submit to narrow instrumentalist thinking.*

Realising that at the end of the PhD pathway *thar be dragons*, I rationalised that writing fiction would serve me better in the long run.

Bad decision, or *Art* decision? *(I will always choose the novel.)*

Philosophy

On New Year's Day (2023) I was surprised by a radio advertisement for Clean Up Australia Day. Once literally and manageably about cleaning up Australia, the annual event is now promoted with an ambitious appeal to *save the planet*. All of our issues have undergone a rapid process of gigantism. We're all Flash Gordon; we all have only '*fourteen hours to save the earth*'.

Likewise, Covid-19 was to the arts what climate change is to pollution; the structural problem overshadowed by the louder problem, so that more insidious issues go unaddressed.

Ensuring the progressive nature of arts problem-solving in the face of a pandemic-sized distraction has been no mean feat. So when Sarah Collins began her 2021 Callaway Lecture by questioning the relationship between arts and economics, she was reinforcing the proposition that the post-pandemic arts economy predicament was not about Covid at all.

SC tenaciously insists we have the opportunity to take art beyond its precarious existence on the periphery of Respect, where it remains persistently on the defensive when it comes to asking for government support. She describes a sector trapped inside the loop of *economism*, and the impossibility of calling for change by deploying the arsenal of immeasurable 'good' attributed to the arts, because '*social cohesion, health and wellbeing, cultural heritage, also often boil down to economics in the context of political discourse*'.

Put more simply, within political-speak the arts – like everything else that has an intrinsic value that cannot and therefore should not be reduced to exclusively economic evaluation – have been reduced to exclusively economic evaluation within contemporary society. Within this cynical and money-driven society politics is ill-equipped to deal with intangible currencies.

Sarah leads us out of what effectively acts as an economics rip by approaching the problem as '*an invitation to think about whether the economism of the current political climate is serving us well, what values underpin it, and whether these values are actually what we want them to be*'.

SC then draws on contemporary trends towards a reinstatement of the aesthetic emphases within 19th Century political economy, which '*viewed production and labour as a function of social relations and historical development*', representing the moment before capitalism changed its ideological course.

Not so coincidentally, a 2022 series within the *Freakonomics* podcast called 'In Search of the Real Adam Smith' – humanist and philosopher – challenges the biblical significance given to selective theories espoused within Adam Smith's *The Wealth of Nations* by champions of free-market ideology. The series examines the strategic neglect of his initial work – *The Theory of Moral Sentiments* – which provides a nuanced philosophical guide designed to mitigate the risks of capitalism spiralling out of control, and failing the public interest.

This return to the source-of-the-problem runs parallel to analyses of the arts sector as it calls for the revision of capitalist ideology, in the name of *wellbeing*. Having acknowledged and appreciated benefits gained through the 'economisation' of the arts in Australia throughout the 1990s (such as *accessibility, anti-elitism)* – whereby the arts were given a quantifiable/measurable formal value based on economic contributions to society – it seems possible now to make that return, in order to also restore Social Value to its rightful place, and refresh where we stand. Combining the best from both worlds would embed art within the body of

Philosophy, where its function can arguably be more fully appreciated and beneficially directed.

Phixing

This is the intellectual climate in which the possibility of an Artist's Living Wage is being considered. The ALW has remarkably become a credible proposition, offering a feasible restoration of values that have been eroded under our increasingly rapacious capitalist system.

An ALW is the only solution that addresses the vast discrepancy between artistic labour and artist income. Returning to Anwen Crawford for her effective summary of the untenable reduction of an artist's worth under capitalism – using the example of authors who are consistently paid *'only a few thousand dollars for books that take them years to write'* – the universal failure of capitalism's value-determination formula is self-evident:

> *To be absolutely clear, I don't think this is a fine state of affairs by any means...*

> *Publishing is not an industry magically exempt – because books! – from the stratification of wealth and resources that defines the rest of life under capitalism. Quite the opposite. Publishing, the music industry, the art world: these largely wage-free zones (for the artist) are in some sense the purest iteration of market logic. The worth of your art is the money it makes when sold – nothing more, nothing less.*

Lauren Carroll Harris's aforementioned 2021 essay 'The Case for Salaried Artists' opens with a summary of four nations that have either piloted ALW-shaped programs, or ingrained ongoing social support for arts workers within formal cultural policy.

LCH uses these teasers towards change as a prompt to discuss the need for ongoing support that elevates creative labour in line with the basic standard of living protected by minimum wages, superannuation and leave entitlements *'other sectors take for granted'*. In doing so she builds upon a vision for social restructuring that would see artists actively involved in emphasising the 'public good' as an acknowledged element of social/cultural exchange.

Problematically, she nonetheless accepts the deferral of the ALW as a distant possibility. Her proposed interim solution links artists to institutions such as galleries, mimicking formal employment arrangements that are likely to benefit a lucky few. This suggests to me that there's no halfway step. Revisioning needs to be dramatic to affect change, which LCH acknowledges herself when she states that *'alone, a strategy for salaried artists at cultural institutions would not be enough'*:

> *The arts cannot flourish without a full reimagining of labour and care. It needs to actively create an economy of belonging for its practitioners – regardless of what is happening in federal politics.*

Many proposed solutions illustrate how hard it is to imagine The Powers That Be will ever give Oliver Twist that second bowl of gruel. Embedded in their *Creativity in Crisis* report, The Australia Institute's proposal of a program that offers 300 three-year fellowships annually, for example, equals a drop in the ocean. Nine hundred practitioners receiving temporary support at any given time doesn't answer the problem of a lifetime of under-paid commitment to their craft. (*How do struggling artists arrive at readiness for these fellowships? What do they return to afterwards? How do arts practitioners who aren't awarded this fellowship survive?)*

And of course, even that inadequate proposal was not adopted within Australia's new National Cultural Policy. A quick glance at the Creative Australia grants pages reveals that only nine fellowships of $80,000 over two years, across nine categories, are being offered. That's just over half the average Australian income being given to arts practitioners described within the conditions as 'outstanding, established artists' (and 'arts workers', with whom the 'outstanding' artists must compete for these fellowships), for 'activity and professional development'.

The trick – so evident in all of these referenced imaginings – is finding the right stepping stones that will take the noble prospect of an ALW from A to B[eing].

Answering the consistent call for activation of the arts within local communities, the Artist's Living Wage offers us a realistic first step in the right direction. With logistical details and [non-competitive] eligibility guidelines to be determined, the leap towards fitting this ideal into a community model is not as impossible as it seems, requiring only that we revise urban and social infrastructure to include secular avenues for meaningful connection.

Sarah Collins concluded her Calllaway lecture by advising against measuring the arts according to current systems of value, insisting instead that *'an arts and cultural policy should be a central component of, and shaping force behind, a national conversation about what type of life we want to lead as a community into the future'*.

Artist-led re-imagining of community models in this direction already exist, so when Barnett, Meyrick and O'Connor ask *'what does re-learning the language of public good look like?'* in their 2021 response to the Australian Institute's *Creativity in Crisis* report (published by *Artshub*), the beginning of an answer is already at hand.

Writer Dave Eggers inspired a niche community movement with his 2008 TED talk 'My Wish: Once Upon a School', which describes his experience in creating 826 Valencia. 826 Valencia is a visionary homework club/tutoring program, designed to address a recognisable need for one-on-one student support that couldn't be met within the under-resourced San Francisco school system. DE organised the real estate by incorporating the program within his existing not-for-profit publishing company (McSweeney's), and encouraged creatives to unite and commit to a volunteer network that would in turn connect them to a broad community, in the service of an achievable ideal. The program became so successful it was adopted by idealistic creative practitioners across the globe, and has since morphed into an ongoing and dynamic series of writing centres that provide a strong foundation for learning.

Expanding upon the already-successful (international) replication of this idea would further answer Barnett/Meyrick/O'Connor's questions about the role of culture in the necessary transformation of society as it faces extreme global crises; *'how can we set culture within a sustainable economic framework built around real needs and public services?'*.

Borrowing from Dave Eggers' Writing Centre model (but moving away from its "unpaid volunteer" character), local Australian councils could create active cultural hubs, within which recipients of the ALW could be mobilised to participate.

Management and staff members of each centre would ideally consist of artists who wish to supplement their basic income or ALW. Creative practitioners could spend their days working within their own practices (home/studio based, or on site), then offer services/support/connection for local youth during "homework club" hours in the afternoons. Coordinated with schools and parents, this would create a structured but informal mentoring model for Australian youth.

With structured adult programs likewise offered in conjunction with existing library services (writing programs, book groups, performances, exhibitions etc.), the centres could provide dynamic, interactive and secular gathering places for entire communities.

This would exemplify the Village raising the Child, but also the Village simply *Being a Village;* a concept in need of revival, to fight the paradoxical loneliness of the connected age.

This Way Phorward

I was finishing secondary school when *Weeping Woman* was kidnapped from the NGV. My creative inclinations have been inadvertently aligned with shifts in cultural understanding since then. The society I live in now wouldn't question the inherent value of a Picasso acquisition. Within a smaller timeframe than three decades, I hope our future society will no longer question why an artist should be paid to thrive in their element.

The development of something like local cultural hubs would animate Sophia Cai's perceived need for artists to *'rethink our current measures of 'success''*. In *Overland,* Andrew Roff's 2018 essay 'Art in a Basic Income Utopia' extends this to further consider how if the arts were embedded naturalistically within diverse communities, *'It would be more difficult to become 'famous' in the current mainstream sense'*, but:

> *Freed from the grasping, sick desperation to 'make it' or fail in a binary way, artists could be more collaborative. We could more confidently carve out niches; engage meaningfully with smaller, self-selecting audiences. Artists would feel more connected, part of a larger web of culture.*

There are many variables to be determined re integrating such a model into the existing cultural environment, but as AR speculates, *'prizes and grants might continue as a means of highlighting and rewarding excellence... but they would not be necessary as a lifeline to support artists who otherwise could not afford to practise'*.

And so, *Dear Tony Burke*, what we required from Australia's new National Cultural Policy was a solution equal to this; one that would have reached the quintessential bottom feeders. Because we know increased funding within the existing system is not the answer to The Arts Problem. The only answer to The Arts Problem is one that allows artists to stay home – or wherever their preferred studio space is – and *make art.*

When The Gimp started referring to himself as an empath and escalated to bald declarations of affection, I would receive endless text messages addressing me as his 'princess' and 'queen'. Enough was enough. I ditched his cliency, because oh you know it, royalty is the enemy of art.

But the damage had been done. My motor tic is Boss and is not going to subside. I now find myself in a new situation, working too few shifts (with less demanding but also less consistent clients) to stabilise, let alone get ahead. Ironically, art and writing might soon be the only things I'm actually able to do. During the months ahead I'll be working inadequate paid hours to enable pure devotion to the multiple projects for which my mind is primed. I'll delay the necessary reckoning for this investment, hoping for my belated "lottery" win.

And like every other artist I'll be trying to answer the question of how to be a grown-up in what has been perceived as a child's profession, performed with crayons leftover from the infancy of our species. This despite already knowing that the progression from cave painting to informed arts practices that engage with complex global social organisation reflects our evolving civilisation[s], each era defined by its literary and visual artefacts, with artists playing an indisputably functional role.

We work outside of certainties, in the fluid world of ideas. We need to be fully-engaged and allowed to fail at times, as part of the process towards success, just as capitalism is failing [us] now, on its way to a better incarnation of itself. This incarnation needs to be determined by people, not The Market – an arbitrary system that was never designed to override the material, emotional and social needs of individuals or the world they inhabit.

For capitalism to obtain a healthy shape, certain things need to exist (protected) outside of the consumer framework. Humanities, the arts, education, housing, healthcare. Environmental management. Human and animal rights. *IMHO.*

When I finally read Ender Baskin's [beautiful] 2021 Judith Wright Poetry Prize winning piece ('are you ready poem'), I find he has young babies and his future dreaming is riddled with ants. He doesn't buy into the Lottery Delusion, calling instead for artists to:

> */ work in league / a common project / get capitalism out of our bones /*

Arts advocacy is happening all around us; economic systems are being critiqued; inspiring books are being read. Heazlewood, Mazzucato, Raworth, even Adam Smith himself, are just a few of many authors who offer new ways forward. Our epiphanies are being weaponised, and we're forging something humanity is on the point of being ready to receive. I can't be imagining this.

Here is your league, Ender Baskan, forming organically in response to a longed-for and now emergent process of change. And so it's with more optimism than bravado that I can say *look out,*

Capitalism, because we're coming for you. En masse we've become a unified force, and possibly the nicest army you could ever hope to meet.

Disclaimer:

The Gimp is a composite of multiple people, whose name and details have been changed to protect his identity. (This makes me slightly less cunty. But not much.)

References

Araluen, Evelyn. (2022, April 29). *2022 Stella Prize Acceptance Speech.* Retrieved from <https://www.youtube.com/watch?v=ub3wTnHSFag>

Barnett, Tully, Meyrick, Julian and O'Connor, Justin. (2021, August 12). 'A New 'Policy Imaginary' for Australian Art and Culture'. *ArtsHub.* Retrieved from <https://www.artshub.com.au/2021/08/12/a-new-policy-imaginary-for-australian-art-and-culture/>

Baskan, Ender. (2022, Autumn). 'are you ready poem'. *Overland,* Issue No. 246. Pp. 70-71.

Burke, Kelly. (2024, October 23). 'Melissa Lucashenko's novel Edenglassie wins $150,000 in book prizes in just 24 hours'. *The Guardian* (Australia Edition). Retrieved from <https://www.theguardian.com/books/2024/oct/23/melissa-lucashenko-edenglassie-book-wins-150000-prizes-awards>

Cai, Sophia. (2022, February 10). 'When Should You Work for Free'. *Art Guide Australia.* Retrieved from <https://artguide.com.au/when-should-you-work-for-free/>

Carroll Harris, Lauren. (2021, August 30). 'The Case for Salaried Artists'. *Kill Your Darlings.* Retrieved from <https://www.killyourdarlings.com.au/article/the-case-for-salaried-artists/>

Collins, Sarah. (2021, December 2). *The Unproductive Arts?: Cultural Economy After Covid* [Radio broadcast]. (2021 Callaway Lecture, Conservatorium of Music, University of Western Australia; recorded 2021, September 4.) *Big Ideas*, ABC Radio National. Retrieved from <https://www.abc.net.au/listen/programs/bigideas/the-cultural-economy-after-covid/13649016>

Commonwealth of Australia. (2023). *Revive: A Place for Every Story, A Story for Every Place – Australia's cultural policy for the next five years*. Retrieved from <https://www.arts.gov.au/what-we-do/new-national-cultural-policy>

Crawford, Anwen. (2022). *Decorum Serves the Rich*. Independently-published zine. Retrieved from <https://demandspopular.net/decorum-serves-the-rich>

Croggon, Alison. (2022, April 16). 'The Campaign to Destroy the Arts'. *The Saturday Paper*, No. 395.

Croggon, Alison. (2019, October). 'The Desertification of Australian Culture'. *The Monthly*.

Dubner, Stephen J. (Host). (2022, December 7). *In Search of the Real Adam Smith* [Audio podcast]. Freakonomics, Episode 525. Produced by Jack Lapinski. Retrieved from <https://freakonomics.com/podcast/in-search-of-the-real-adam-smith/>

Eggers, Dave. (2008, February). *My Wish: Once Upon a School* [Video]. TED Conferences. Retrieved from <https://www.ted.com/talks/dave_eggers_my_wish_once_upon_a_school?subtitle=en>

Eltham, Ben and Pennington, Alison. (2021, July). *Creativity in Crisis: Rebooting Australia's Arts and Entertainment Sector After Covid.* The Centre for Future Work at The Australia Institute. Retrieved from <https://futurework.org.au/report/creativity-in-crisis-rebooting-australias-arts-and-entertainment-sector-after-covid/>

Hitchens, Christopher. (2008). *God is Not Great: How Religion Poisons Everything.* Allen & Unwin.

Fennel, Mark (Dir). (2021, December). *Framed: Australia's Greatest Art Heist.* Produced by *The Feed.* SBS on Demand.

Georgiou, Marisa. (2023, July 31). 'Artist burnout is not a mental health issue it is a labour issue'. *ArtsHub News.* Retrieved from <https://www.artshub.com.au/news/opinions-analysis/artist-burnout-is-not-a-mental-health-issue-it-is-a-labour-issue-2650825/>

Heazlewood, Justin. (2014). *Funemployed: Life as an Artist in Australia.* Affirm Press, South Melbourne.

Hodges, Mike (Dir.). (1980). *Flash Gordon.* Starling Films, USA.

Ley, James. (2022). 'Trapped in Negation'. *Open Secrets: Essays on the Writing Life,* Ed. Catriona Menzies-Pike. Sydney Review of Books.

Lucashenko, Melissa. (2024). *Edenglassie.* University of Queensland Press.

Luckman, Susan and Taylor, Stephanie. (2024). 'There's a lot of luck involved': Sustaining hope labour amid workplace inequality and precarity as a creative worker'. *Cuadernos de Relaciones Laborales,* 42 (1). PP. 59-72. DOI: 10.5209/crla.91566. Retrieved from <https://oro.open.ac.uk/96808/1/Luckman%20and%20Taylor%20 2024%20Sustaining%20hope%20labour.pdf>

Mazzucato, Mariana. (2018). *The Value of Everything: Makers and Takers in the Global Economy*. Penguin Books Ltd.

Mills, Jennifer. (2021, November 22). 'Precarious Words'. *Overland*. Retrieved from <https://overland.org.au/2021/11/precarious-words/>

Raworth, Kate. (2018). *Doughnut Economics: Seven Ways to Think Like a 21st-Century Economist*. Random House.

Roff, Andrew. (2018, January 24). 'Art in a Basic Income Utopia'. *Overland*. Retrieved from <https://overland.org.au/2018/01/art-in-a-basic-income-utopia/>

Sanadze, Nina. (2020, July 29). *Living Room Series: Christine Fontana* [Video]. Retrieved from <https://www.youtube.com/watch?v=kLsxxLAF3JE>

Smith, Adam. (2008). *An Inquiry into the Nature and Causes of the Wealth of Nations*. Oxford University Press. (Original work published 1776)

Smith, Adam. (2010). *The Theory of Moral Sentiments*. Penguin Classics. (Original work published 1759)

Wood, Charlotte. (2022). New National Cultural Policy Submission; ncp0136_charlotte-wood. Retrieved from <https://www.arts.gov.au/sites/default/files/documents/ncp0136_charlotte-wood.pdf>

Woolf, Virginia. (1977). *A Room of One's Own*. Grafton Books, London. (Original work published 1929)

www.ingramcontent.com/pod-product-compliance
Lightning Source LLC
LaVergne TN
LVHW050939210926
848482LV00013B/669
* 9 7 8 1 9 2 3 2 2 1 0 1 7 *